*THE FABER LIBRARY—No. 55*

# THE LISTENERS, AND OTHER POEMS

Poetry by Walter de la Mare

———

*Memory*

*The Fleeting*

*The Veil*

*Motley*

*The Listeners*

*Collected Poems*

———

*Ding Dong Bell*

———

*Songs of Childhood*

*Stuff and Nonsense*

*Bells and Grass*

*Peacock Pie*

*This Year, Next Year*

# WALTER
# DE LA MARE

---

# THE LISTENERS
## *and other poems*

FABER AND FABER LIMITED
24 Russell Square
London

First published in this new edition Mcmxlii
by Faber and Faber Limited
24 Russell Square London W.C.1
Printed in Great Britain
at the Bowering Press Plymouth
All Rights reserved

The wood-engraving on the title-page
is by Reynolds Stone

# CONTENTS

5

# Contents

# Contents

# The Three Cherry Trees

There were three cherry trees once,
  Grew in a garden all shady;
And there for delight of so gladsome a sight,
  Walked a most beautiful lady,
  Dreamed a most beautiful lady.

Birds in those branches did sing,
  Blackbird and throstle and linnet,
But she walking there was by far the most fair—
  Lovelier than all else within it,
  Blackbird and throstle and linnet.

But blossoms to berries do come,
  All hanging on stalks light and slender,
And one long summer's day charmed that lady away,
  With vows sweet and merry and tender;
  A lover with voice low and tender.

Moss and lichen the green branches deck;
  Weeds nod in its paths green and shady:
Yet a light footstep seems there to wander in dreams,
  The ghost of that beautiful lady,
  That happy and beautiful lady.

# Old Susan

When Susan's work was done she'd sit,
With one fat guttering candle lit,
And window opened wide to win
The sweet night air to enter in;
There, with a thumb to keep her place
She'd read, with stern and wrinkled face,
Her mild eyes gliding very slow
Across the letters to and fro,
While wagged the guttering candle flame
In the wind that through the window came.
And sometimes in the silence she
Would mumble a sentence audibly,
Or shake her head as if to say,
'You silly souls, to act this way!'
And never a sound from night I'd hear,
Unless some far-off cock crowed clear;
Or her old shuffling thumb should turn
Another page; and rapt and stern,
Through her great glasses bent on me
She'd glance into reality;
And shake her round old silvery head,
With—'You!—I thought you was in bed!'—
Only to tilt her book again,
And rooted in Romance remain.

# Old Ben

Sad is old Ben Thistlewaite,
  Now his day is done,
And all his children
  Far away are gone.

He sits beneath his jasmined porch,
  His stick between his knees,
His eyes fixed vacant
  On his moss-grown trees.

Grass springs in the green path,
  His flowers are lean and dry,
His thatch hangs in wisps against
  The evening sky.

He has no heart to care now,
  Though the winds will blow
Whistling in his casement,
  And the rain drip thro'.

He thinks of his old Bettie,
  How she'd shake her head and say,
'You'll live to wish my sharp old tongue
  Could scold—some day.'

But as in pale high autumn skies
  The swallows float and play,
His restless thoughts pass to and fro,
  But nowhere stay.

Soft, on the morrow, they are gone,
  His garden then will be
Denser and shadier and greener,
  Greener the moss-grown tree.

# Miss Loo

When thin-strewn memory I look through,
I see most clearly poor Miss Loo,
Her tabby cat, her cage of birds,
Her nose, her hair—her muffled words,
And how she'd open her green eyes,
As if in some immense surprise,
Whenever as we sat at tea
She made some small remark to me.

It's always drowsy summer when
From out the past she comes again;
The westering sunshine in a pool
Floats in her parlour still and cool;
While the slim bird its lean wires shakes,
As into piercing song it breaks;
Till Peter's pale-green eyes ajar
Dream, wake; wake, dream, in one brief bar.

And I am sitting, dull and shy,
And she with gaze of vacancy,
And large hands folded on the tray,
Musing the afternoon away;
Her satin bosom heaving slow
With sighs that softly ebb and flow,
And her plain face in such dismay,
It seems unkind to look her way:
Until all cheerful back will come
Her cheerful gleaming spirit home:
And one would think that poor Miss Loo
Asked nothing else, if she had you.

# The Tailor

Few footsteps stray when dusk droops o'er
The tailor's old stone-lintelled door:
There sits he stitching half asleep,
Beside his smoky tallow dip.
'Click, click,' his needle hastes, and shrill
Cries back the cricket 'neath the sill.
Sometimes he stays, and o'er his thread
Leans sidelong his old tousled head;
Or stoops to peer with half-shut eye
When some strange footfall echoes by;
Till clearer gleams his candle's spark
Into the dusty summer dark.
Then from his crosslegs he gets down,
To find how dark the evening's grown;
And hunched-up in his door he'll hear
The cricket whistling crisp and clear;
And so beneath the starry grey
Will mutter half a seam away.

# Martha

'Once . . . once upon a time . . .'
  Over and over again,
Martha would tell us her stories,
  In the hazel glen.

Hers were those clear grey eyes
  You watch, and the story seems
Told by their beautifulness
  Tranquil as dreams.

She'd sit with her two slim hands
  Clasped round her bended knees;
While we on our elbows lolled,
  And stared at ease.

Her voice and her narrow chin,
  Her grave small lovely head,
Seemed half the meaning.
  Of the words she said.

'Once . . . once upon a time . . .'
  Like a dream you dream in the night,
Fairies and gnomes stole out
  In the leaf-green light.

And her beauty far away
  Would fade, as her voice ran on,
Till hazel and summer sun
  And all were gone:—

All fordone and forgot;
   And like clouds in the height of the sky,
Our hearts stood still in the hush
   Of an age gone by.

# The Sleeper

As Ann came in one summer's day,
  She felt that she must creep,
So silent was the clear cool house,
  It seemed a house of sleep.
And sure, when she pushed open the door,
  Rapt in the stillness there,
Her mother sat, with stooping head,
  Asleep upon a chair;
Fast—fast asleep; her two hands laid
  Loose-folded on her knee,
So that her small unconscious face
  Looked half unreal to be:
So calmly lit with sleep's pale light
  Each feature was; so fair
Her forehead—every trouble was
  Smoothed out beneath her hair.

But though her mind in dream now moved,
  Still seemed her gaze to rest
From out beneath her fast-sealed lids,
  Above her moving breast,
On Ann, as quite, quite still she stood;
  Yet slumber lay so deep
Even her hands upon her lap
  Seemed saturate with sleep.
And as Ann peeped, a cloudlike dread
  Stole over her, and then,
On stealthy, mouselike feet she trod,
  And tiptoed out again.

# The Keys of Morning

While at her bedroom window once,
  Learning her task for school,
Little Louisa lonely sat
  In the morning clear and cool,
She slanted her small bead-brown eyes
  Across the empty street,
And saw Death softly watching her
  In the sunshine pale and sweet.
His was a long lean sallow face,
  He sat with half-shut eyes,
Like an old sailor in a ship
  Becalmed 'neath tropic skies.
Beside him in the dust he'd set
  His staff and shady hat;
These, peeping small, Louisa saw
  Quite clearly where she sat—

The thinness of his coal-black locks,
  His hands so long and lean
They scarcely seemed to grasp at all
  The keys that hung between:
Both were of gold, but one was small,
  And with this last did he
Wag in the air, as if to say,
  'Come hither, child, to me!'

Louisa laid her lesson book
  On the cold window-sill;
And in the sleepy sunshine house
  Went softly down, until

She stood in the half-opened door,
   And peeped; but strange to say,
Where Death just now had sunning sat
   Only a shadow lay—
Just the tall chimney's round-topped cowl,
   And the small sun behind,
Had with its shadow in the dust
   Called sleepy Death to mind.
But most she thought how strange it was
   Two keys that he should bear,
And that, when beckoning, he should wag
   The littlest in the air.

# Rachel

Rachel sings sweet—
　Oh yes, at night,
Her pale face bent
　In the candle-light,
Her slim hands touch
　The answering keys,
And she sings of hope
　And of memories:
Sings to the little
　Boy that stands
Watching those slim,
　Light, heedful hands.
He looks in her face;
　Her dark eyes seem
Dark with a beautiful
　Distant dream;
And still she plays,
　Sings tenderly
To him of hope,
　And of memory.

# Alone

A very old woman
Lives in yon house—
The squeak of the cricket,
The stir of the mouse,
Are all she knows
Of the earth and us.

Once she was young,
Would dance and play,
Like many another
Young popinjay;
And run to her mother
At dusk of day.

And colours bright
She delighted in;
The fiddle to hear,
And to lift her chin,
And sing as small
As a twittering wren.

But age apace
Comes at last to all;
And a lone house filled
With the cricket's call;
And the scampering mouse
In the hollow wall.

# The Bells

Shadow and light both strove to be
The eight bell-ringers' company,
As with his gliding rope in hand,
Counting his changes, each did stand;
While rang and trembled every stone,
To music by the bell-mouths blown,
Till the bright clouds that towered on high
Seemed to re-echo cry with cry.
Still swang the clappers to and fro,
When, in the far-spread fields below,
I saw a ploughman with his team
Lift to the bells and fix on them
His distant eyes, as if he would
Drink in the utmost sound he could;
While near him sat his children three,
And in the green grass placidly
Played undistracted on, as if
What music earthly bells might give
Could only faintly stir their dream,
And stillness make more lovely seem.

Soon night hid horses, children, all
In sleep deep and ambrosial;
Yet, yet it seemed from star to star,
Welling now near, now faint and far,
Those echoing bells rang on in dream,
And stillness made even lovelier seem.

# The Scarecrow

All winter through I bow my head
  Beneath the driving rain;
The North wind powders me with snow
  And blows me black again;
At midnight 'neath a maze of stars
  I flame with glittering rime,
And stand, above the stubble, stiff
  As mail at morning-prime.
But when that child, called Spring, and all
  His host of children, come,
Scattering their buds and dew upon
  These acres of my home,
Some rapture in my rags awakes;
  I lift void eyes and scan
The skies for crows, those ravening foes,
  Of my strange master, Man.
I watch him striding lank behind
  His clashing team, and know
Soon will the wheat swish body high
  Where once lay sterile snow;
Soon shall I gaze across a sea
  Of sun-begotten grain,
Which my unflinching watch hath sealed
  For harvest once again.

# Nod

Softly along the road of evening,
    In a twilight dim with rose,
Wrinkled with age, and drenched with dew,
    Old Nod, the shepherd, goes.

His drowsy flock streams on before him,
    Their fleeces charged with gold,
To where the sun's last beam leans low
    On Nod the shepherd's fold.

The hedge is quick and green with brier,
    From their sand the conies creep;
And all the birds that fly in heaven
    Flock singing home to sleep.

His lambs outnumber a noon's roses,
    Yet, when night's shadows fall,
His blind old sheep-dog, Slumber-soon,
    Misses not one of all.

His are the quiet steeps of dreamland,
    The waters of no-more-pain,
His ram's bell rings 'neath an arch of stars,
    'Rest, rest; and rest again.'

# The Bindweed

The bindweed roots pierce down
Deeper than men do lie,
Laid in their dark-shut graves
Their slumbering kinsmen by.

Yet what frail thin-spun flowers
She casts into the air,
To breathe the sunshine, and
To leave her fragrance there.

But when the sweet moon comes,
Showering her silver down,
Half-wreathèd in faint sleep,
They droop where they have blown.

So all the grass is set,
Beneath her trembling ray,
With buds that have been flowers,
Brimmed with reflected day.

# Winter

Clouded with snow
　The cold winds blow,
And shrill on leafless bough
The robin with its burning breast
　Alone sings now.

　The rayless sun,
　Day's journey done,
Sheds its last ebbing light
On fields in leagues of beauty spread
　Unearthly white.

　Thick draws the dark,
　And spark by spark,
The frost-fires kindle, and soon
Over that sea of frozen foam
　Floats the white moon.

# There Blooms no Bud in May

There blooms no bud in May
Can for its white compare
With snow at break of day,
On fields forlorn and bare.

For shadow it hath rose,
Azure, and amethyst;
And every air that blows
Dies out in beauteous mist.

It hangs the frozen bough
With flowers on which the night
Wheeling her darkness through
Scatters a starry light.

Fearful of its pale glare
In flocks the starlings rise;
Slide through the frosty air,
And perch with plaintive cries.

Only the inky rook,
Hunched cold in ruffled wings,
Its snowy nest forsook,
Caws of unnumbered Springs.

# Noon and Night Flower

Not any flower that blows
　But shining watch doth keep;
Every swift changing chequered hour it knows
Now to break forth in beauty; now to sleep.

This for the roving bee
　Keeps open house, and this
Stainless and clear is, that in darkness she
May lure the moth to where her nectar is.

Lovely beyond the rest
　Are these of all delight:—
The tiny pimpernel that noon loves best,
The primrose palely burning through the night.

One 'neath day's burning sky
　With ruby decks her place,
The other when Eve's chariot glideth by
Lifts her dim torch to light that dreaming face.

# Estranged

No one was with me there—
Happy I was—alone;
Yet from the sunshine suddenly
   A joy was gone.

A bird in an empty house
Sad echoes makes to ring,
Flitting from room to room
   On restless wing:

Till from its shades he flies,
And leaves forlorn and dim
The narrow solitudes
   So strange to him.

So, when with fickle heart
I joyed in the passing day,
A presence my mood estranged
   Went grieved away.

# The Tired Cupid

The thin moonlight with trickling ray,
Thridding the boughs of silver may,
Trembles in beauty, pale and cool,
On folded flower, and mantled pool.
All in a haze the rushes lean—
And he—he sits, with chin between
His two cold hands; his bare feet set
Deep in the grasses, green and wet.
About his head a hundred rings
Of gold loop down to meet his wings,
Whose feathers, arched their stillness through,
Gleam with slow-gathering drops of dew.
The mouse-bat peers; the stealthy vole
Creeps from the covert of its hole;
A shimmering moth its pinions furls,
Grey in the moonshine of his curls;
'Neath the faint stars the night-airs stray,
Scattering the fragrance of the may;
And with each stirring of the bough
Shadow beclouds his childlike brow.

# Dreams

Be gentle, O hands of a child;
Be true: like a shadowy sea
In the starry darkness of night
   Are your eyes to me.

But words are shallow, and soon
Dreams fade that the heart once knew;
And youth fades out in the mind,
   In the dark eyes too.

What can a tired heart say,
Which the wise of the world have made dumb?
Save to the lonely dreams of a child,
   'Return again, come!'

## Faithless

The words you said grow faint;
The lamp you lit burns dim;
Yet, still be near your faithless friend
To urge and counsel him.

Still with returning feet
To where life's shadows brood,
With steadfast eyes made clear in death
Haunt his vague solitude.

So he, beguiled with earth,
Yet with its vain things vexed,
Keep even to his own heart unknown
Your memory unperplexed.

# The Shade

Darker than night; and oh, much darker, she,
Whose eyes in deep night darkness gaze on me.
No stars surround her; yet the moon seems hid
Afar somewhere, beneath that narrow lid.
She darkens against the darkness; and her face
Only by adding thought to thought I trace,
Limned shadowily: O dream, return once more
To gloomy Hades and the whispering shore!

# Be Angry Now No More

Be angry now no more!
If I have grieved thee—if
Thy kindness, mine before,
No hope may now restore:
Only forgive, forgive!

If still resentment burns
In thy cold breast, oh if
No more to pity turns,
No more, once tender, yearns
Thy love; oh yet forgive! . . .

Ask of the winter rain
June's withered rose again:
Ask grace of the salt sea:
She will not answer thee.
God would ten times have shriven
A heart so riven;
In her cold care thou'd'st be
Still unforgiven.

# Spring

Once when my life was young,
I, too, with Spring's bright face
By mine, walked softly along,
   Pace to his pace.

Then burned his crimson may,
Like a clear flame outspread,
Arching our happy way:
   Then would he shed

Strangely from his wild face
Wonderful light on me—
Like hounds that keen in chase
   Their quarry see.

Oh, sorrow now to know
What shafts, what keenness cold
His are to pierce me through,
   Now that I'm old.

# Exile

Had the gods loved me I had lain
    Where darnel is, and thorn,
And the wild night-bird's nightlong strain
    Trembles in boughs forlorn.

Nay, but they loved me not; and I
    Must needs a stranger be,
Whose every exiled day gone by
    Aches with their memory.

# Where?

Where is my love—
  In silence and shadow she lies,
Under the April-grey, calm waste of the skies;
    And a bird above,
  In the darkness tender and clear,
Keeps saying over and over, Love lies here!

  Not that's she dead;
  Only her soul is flown
Out of its last pure earthly mansion;
    And cries instead
  In the darkness, tender and clear,
Like the voice of a bird in the leaves, Love—love lies
      here.

# Music Unheard

Sweet sounds, begone—
Whose music on my ear
Stirs foolish discontent
Of lingering here;
When, if I crossed
The crystal verge of death,
Him I should see
Who these sounds murmureth

Sweet sounds, begone—
Ask not my heart to break
Its bond of bravery for
Sweet quiet's sake;
Lure not my feet
To leave the path they must
Tread on, unfaltering,
Till I sleep in dust.

Sweet sounds, begone:
Though silence brings apace
Deadly disquiet
Of this homeless place;
And all I love
In beauty cries to me,
'We but vain shadows
And reflections be.'

# All That's Past

Very old are the woods;
　And the buds that break
Out of the briar's boughs,
　When March winds wake,
So old with their beauty are—
　Oh, no man knows
Through what wild centuries
　Roves back the rose.

Very old are the brooks;
　And the rills that rise
Where snow sleeps cold beneath
　The azure skies
Sing such a history
　Of come and gone,
Their every drop is as wise
　As Solomon.

Very old are we men;
　Our dreams are tales
Told in dim Eden
　By Eve's nightingales;
We wake and whisper awhile,
　But, the day gone by,
Silence and sleep like fields
　Of amaranth lie.

# When the Rose is Faded

When the rose is faded,
Memory may still dwell on
Her beauty shadowed,
And the sweet smell gone.

That vanishing loveliness,
That burdening breath
No bond of life hath then
Nor grief of death.

'Tis the immortal thought
Whose passion still
Makes of the changing
The unchangeable.

Oh, thus thy beauty,
Loveliest on earth to me,
Dark with no sorrow, shines
And burns, with Thee.

# Sleep

Men all, and birds, and creeping beasts,
When the dark of night is deep,
From the moving wonder of their lives
Commit themselves to sleep.

Without a thought, or fear, they shut
The narrow gates of sense;
Heedless and quiet, in slumber turn
Their strength to impotence.

The transient strangeness of the earth
Their spirits no more see;
Within a silent gloom withdrawn,
They slumber in secrecy.

Two worlds they have—a globe forgot
Wheeling from dark to light;
And all the enchanted realm of dream
That burgeons out of night.

# The Stranger

Half-hidden in a graveyard,
  In the blackness of a yew,
Where never living creature stirs,
  Nor sunbeam pierces through,

Is a tombstone green and crooked,
  Its faded legend gone,
And but one rain-worn cherub's head
  To sing of the unknown.

There, when the dusk is falling,
  Silence broods so deep
It seems that every wind that breathes
  Blows from the fields of sleep.

Day breaks in heedless beauty,
  Kindling each drop of dew,
But unforsaking shadow dwells
  Beneath this lonely yew.

And, all else lost and faded,
  Only this listening head
Keeps with a strange unanswering smile
  Its secret with the dead.

# Never More, Sailor

Never more, Sailor,
Shalt thou be
Tossed on the wind-ridden,
Restless sea.
Its tides may labour;
All the world
Shake 'neath that weight
Of waters hurled:
But its whole shock
Can only stir
Thy dust to a quiet
Even quieter.
Thou mock'd'st at land
Who now art come
To such a small
And shallow home;
Yet bore the sea
Full many a care
For bones that once
A sailor's were.
And though the grave's
Deep soundlessness
Thy once sea-deafened
Ear distress,
No robin ever
On the deep
Hopped with his song
To haunt thy sleep.

# The Witch

Weary went the old Witch,
Weary of her pack,
She sat her down by the churchyard wall,
And jerked it off her back.

The cord brake, yes, the cord brake,
Just where the dead did lie,
And Charms and Spells and Sorceries
Spilled out beneath the sky.

Weary was the old Witch;
She rested her old eyes
From the lantern-fruited yew trees,
And the scarlet of the skies;

And out the dead came stumbling,
From every rift and crack,
Silent as moss, and plundered
The gaping pack.

They wish them, three times over,
Away they skip full soon:
Bat and Mole and Leveret,
Under the rising moon;

Owl and Newt and Nightjar:
They take their shapes and creep,
Silent as churchyard lichen,
While she squats asleep.

All of these dead were stirring:
Each unto each did call,
'A Witch, a Witch is sleeping
Under the churchyard wall;

'A Witch, a Witch is sleeping . . .'
The shrillness ebbed away;
And up the way-worn moon clomb bright,
Hard on the track of day.

She shone, high, wan and silvery;
Day's colours paled and died:
And, save the mute and creeping worm,
Nought else was there beside.

Names may be writ; and mounds rise;
Purporting, Here be bones:
But empty is that churchyard
Of all save stones.

Owl and Newt and Nightjar,
Leveret, Bat and Mole
Haunt and call in the twilight,
Where she slept, poor soul.

# Arabia

Far are the shades of Arabia,
Where the Princes ride at noon,
'Mid the verdurous vales and thickets,
Under the ghost of the moon;
And so dark is that vaulted purple
Flowers in the forest rise
And toss into blossom 'gainst the phantom stars
Pale in the noonday skies.

Sweet is the music of Arabia
In my heart, when out of dreams
I still in the thin clear mirk of dawn
Descry her gliding streams;
Hear her strange lutes on the green banks
Ring loud with the grief and delight
Of the dim-silked, dark-haired Musicians
In the brooding silence of night.

They haunt me—her lutes and her forests;
No beauty on earth I see
But shadowed with that dream recalls
Her loveliness to me:
Still eyes look coldly upon me,
Cold voices whisper and say—
'He is crazed with the spell of far Arabia,
They have stolen his wits away.'

# The Mountains

Still, and blanched, and cold, and lone,
The icy hills far off from me
With frosty ulys overgrown
Stand in their sculptured secrecy.

No path of theirs the chamois fleet
Treads, with a nostril to the wind;
O'er their ice-marbled glaciers beat
No wings of eagles in my mind—

Yea, in my mind these mountains rise,
Their perils dyed with evening's rose;
And still my ghost sits at my eyes
And thirsts for their untroubled snows.

# Queen Djenira

When Queen Djenira slumbers through
   The sultry noon's repose,
From out her dreams, as soft she lies,
   A faint thin music flows.

Her lovely hands lie narrow and pale
   With gilded nails, her head
Couched in its banded nets of gold
   Lies pillowed on her bed.

The little Nubian boys who fan
   Her cheeks and tresses clear,
Wonderful, wonderful, wonderful voices
   Seem afar to hear.

They slide their eyes, and nodding, say,
   'Queen Djenira walks to-day
The courts of the lord Pthamasar
   Where the sweet birds of Psuthys are.'

And those of earth about her porch
   Of shadow cool and grey
Their sidelong beaks in silence lean,
   And silent flit away.

# Never-to-Be

Down by the waters of the sea,
Reigns the King of Never-to-be.
His palace walls are black with night;
His torches star and moonès light,
And for his timepiece deep and grave
Beats on the green unhastening wave.

Windswept are his high corridors;
His pleasance the sea-mantled shores;
For sentinel a shadow stands
With hair in heaven, and cloudy hands;
And round his bed, king's guards to be,
Watch pines in iron solemnity.

His hound is mute; his steed at will
Roams pastures deep with asphodel;
His queen is to her slumber gone;
His courtiers mute lie, hewn in stone;
He hath forgot where he did hide
His sceptre in the mountain-side.

Grey-capped and muttering, mad is he—
The childless King of Never-to-be;
For all his people in the deep
Keep everlasting fast asleep;
And all his realm is foam and rain,
Whispering of what comes not again.

# The Dark Château

In dreams a dark château
    Stands ever open to me,
In far ravines dream-waters flow,
    Descending soundlessly;
Above its peaks the eagle floats,
    Lone in a sunless sky;
Mute are the golden woodland throats
    Of the birds flitting by.

No voice is audible.  The wind
    Sleeps in its peace.
No flower of the light can find
    Refuge 'neath its trees;
Only the darkening ivy climbs
    Mingled with wilding rose,
And cypress, morn and evening, time's
    Black shadow throws.

All vacant, and unknown;
    Only the dreamer steps
From stone to hollow stone,
    Where the green moss sleeps,
Peers at the river in its deeps,
    The eagle lone in the sky,
While the dew of evening drips,
    Coldly and silently.

Would that I could press in!—
    Into each secret room;

Would that my sleep-bright eyes could win
    To the inner gloom;
Gaze from its high windows,
    Far down its mouldering walls,
Where amber-clear still Lethe flows,
    And foaming falls.

But ever as I gaze,
    From slumber soft doth come
Some touch my stagnant sense to raise
    To its old earthly home;
Fades then that sky serene;
    And peak of ageless snow;
Fades to a paling dawn-lit green,
    My dark château.

# The Dwelling-Place

Deep in a forest where the kestrel screamed,
Beside a lake of water, clear as glass,
The time-worn windows of a stone house gleamed,
      Named only 'Alas.'

Yet happy as the wild birds in the glades
Of that green forest, thridding the still air
With low continued heedless serenades,
      Its heedless people were.

The throbbing chords of violin and lute,
The lustre of lean tapers in dark eyes,
Fair colours, beauteous flowers, dainty fruit
      Made earth seem Paradise

To them that dwelt within this lonely house:
Like children of the gods in lasting peace,
They ate, sang, danced, as if each day's carouse
      Need never pause, nor cease.

Some might cry, Vanity! to a weeping lyre,
Some in that deep pool mock their longings vain,
Came yet at last long silence to the wire,
      And dark did dark remain.

Some to the hunt would wend, with hound and horn,
And clash of silver, beauty, bravery, pride,
Heeding not one who on white horse upborne
      With soundless hoofs did ride.

Dreamers there were who watched the hours away
Beside a fountain's foam. And in the sweet
Of phantom evening, 'neath the night-bird's lay,
      Did loved with loved-one meet.

All, all were children, for, the long day done,
They barred the heavy door 'gainst lightfoot fear; —
And few words spake though one known face was gone,
      Yet still seemed hovering near.

They heaped the bright fire higher; poured dark wine;
And in long revelry dazed the questioning eye;
Curtained three-fold the heart-dismaying shine
      Of midnight streaming by.

They shut the dark out from the painted wall,
With candles dared the shadow at the door,
Sang down the faint reiterated call
      Of those who came no more.

Yet clear above that portal plain was writ,
Confronting each at length alone to pass
Out of its beauty into night star-lit,
      That worn 'Alas!'

# The Listeners

'Is there anybody there?' said the Traveller,
  Knocking on the moonlit door;
And his horse in the silence champed the grasses
  Of the forest's ferny floor;
And a bird flew up out of the turret,
  Above the Traveller's head:
And he smote upon the door again a second time;
  'Is there anybody there?' he said.
But no-one descended to the Traveller;
  No head from the leaf-fringed sill
Leaned over and looked into his grey eyes,
  Where he stood perplexed and still.
But only a host of phantom listeners
  That dwelt in the lone house then
Stood listening in the quiet of the moonlight
  To that voice from the world of men:
Stood thronging the faint moonbeams on the dark stair,
  That goes down to the empty hall,
Hearkening in an air stirred and shaken
  By the lonely Traveller's call.
And he felt in his heart their strangeness,
  Their stillness answering his cry,
While his horse moved, cropping the dark turf,
  'Neath the starred and leafy sky;
For he suddenly smote on the door, even
  Louder, and lifted his head:—
'Tell them I came, and no-one answered,
  That I kept my word,' he said.
Never the least stir made the listeners,
  Though every word he spake

Fell echoing through the shadowiness of the still house
    From the one man left awake:
Ay, they heard his foot upon the stirrup,
    And the sound of iron on stone,
And how the silence surged softly backward,
    When the plunging hoofs were gone.

# Time Passes

There was nought in the Valley
But a Tower of Ivory,
Its base enwreathed with red
Flowers that at evening
Caught the sun's crimson
As to Ocean low he sped.

Lucent and lovely
It stood in the morning
Under a trackless hill;
With snows eternal
Muffling its summit,
And silence ineffable.

Sighing of solitude
Winds from the cold heights
Haunted its yellowing stone;
At noon its shadow
Stretched athwart cedars
Whence every bird was flown.

Its stair was broken,
Its starlit walls were
Fretted; its flowers shone
Wide at the portal,
Full-blown and fading,
Their last faint fragrance gone.

And on high in its lantern
A shape of the living

Watched o'er a shoreless sea,
From a Tower rotting
With age and weakness,
Once lovely as ivory.

# Beware!

An ominous bird sang from its branch,
    'Beware, O Wanderer!
Night 'mid her flowers of glamourie spilled
    Draws swiftly near:

'Night with her darkened caravans,
    Piled deep with silver and myrrh,
Draws from the portals of the East,
    O Wanderer near!

'Night who walks plumèd through the fields
    Of stars that strangely stir—
Smitten to fire by the sandals of him
    Who walks with her.'

# The Journey

Heart-sick of his journey was the Wanderer;
    Footsore and sad was he;
And a Witch who long had lurked by the wayside,
    Looked out of sorcery.

'Lift up your eyes, you lonely Wanderer,'
    She peeped from her casement small;
'Here's shelter and quiet to give you rest, young man,
    And apples for thirst withal.'

And he looked up out of his sad reverie,
    And saw all the woods in green,
With birds that flitted feathered in the dappling,
    The jewel-bright leaves between.

And he lifted up his face towards her lattice,
    And there, alluring-wise,
Slanting through the silence of the long past,
    Dwelt the still green Witch's eyes.

And vaguely from the hiding-place of memory
    Voices seemed to cry:
'What is the darkness of one brief life-time
    To the deaths thou hast made us die?

'Heed not the words of the Enchantress
    Who would us still betray!'
And sad with the echo of their reproaches,
    Doubting, he turned away.

'I may not shelter 'neath your roof, lady,
    Nor in this wood's green shadow seek repose,
Nor will your apples quench the thirst
    A homesick wanderer knows.'

' "Homesick," forsooth!' she softly mocked him:
    And the beauty in her face
Made in the sunshine pale and trembling
    A stillness in that place.

And he sighed, as if in fear, the young Wanderer,
    Looking to left and to right,
Where the endless narrow road swept onward,
    In the distance lost to sight.

And there fell upon his sense the briar,
    Haunting the air with its breath,
And the faint shrill sweetness of the birds' throats,
    Their tent of leaves beneath.

And there was the Witch, in no wise heeding;
    Her arbour, and fruit-filled dish,
Her pitcher of well-water, and clear damask—
    All that the weary wish.

And the last gold beam across the green world
    Faltered and failed, as he
Remembered his solitude and the dark night's
    Inhospitality.

His shoulders were bowed with his knapsack;
    His staff trailed heavy in the dust;

His eyes were dazed, and hopeless of the white road
  Which tread all pilgrims must.

And he looked upon the Witch with eyes of sorrow
  In the darkening of the day;
And turned him aside into oblivion;
  And the voices died away. . . .

And the Witch stepped down from her casement:
  In the hush of night he heard
The calling and wailing in dewy thicket
  Of bird to hidden bird.

And gloom stole all her burning crimson,
  Remote and faint in space
As stars in gathering shadow of the evening
  Seemed now her phantom face.

And one night's rest shall be a myriad,
  Midst dreams that come and go;
Till heedless fate, unmoved by weakness, bring him
  This same strange by-way through:

To the beauty of earth that fades in ashes,
  The lips of welcome, and the eyes
More beauteous than the feeble shine of Hesper
  Lone in the lightening skies:

Till once again the Witch's guile entreat him;
  But, worn with wisdom, he
Steadfast and cold shall choose the dark night's
  Inhospitality.

# Haunted

The rabbit in his burrow keeps
No guarded watch, in peace he sleeps;
The wolf that howls into the night
Cowers to her lair at morning light;
The simplest bird entwines a nest
Where she may lean her lovely breast,
Couched in the silence of the bough;
But thou, O man, what rest hast thou?

The deepest solitude can bring
Only a subtler questioning
In thy divided heart; thy bed
Recalls at dawn what midnight said;
Seek how thou wilt to feign content
Thy flaming ardour's quickly spent;
Soon thy last company is gone,
And leaves thee—with thyself—alone.

Pomp and great friends may hem thee round,
A thousand busy tasks be found;
Earth's thronging beauties may beguile
Thy longing lovesick heart awhile;
And pride, like clouds of sunset, spread
A changing glory round thy head;
But fade will all; and thou must come,
Hating thy journey, homeless, home.

Rave how thou wilt; unmoved, remote,
That inward presence slumbers not,

Frets out each secret from thy breast,
Gives thee no rally, pause, nor rest,
Scans close thy very thoughts, lest they
Should sap his patient power away,
Answers thy wrath with peace, thy cry
With tenderest taciturnity.

# Silence

With changeful sound life beats upon the ear;
   Yet striving for release
   The most delighting string's
     Sweet jargonings,
     The happiest throat's
   Most easeful, lovely notes
Fall back into a veiling silentness.

Even 'mid the rumour of a moving host,
   Blackening the clear green earth,
   Vainly 'gainst that thin wall
     The trumpets call,
     Or with loud hum
   The smoke-bemuffled drum:
From that high quietness no reply comes forth.

When all at peace, two friends at ease alone
   Talk out their hearts,—yet still,
   Between the grace-notes of
     The voice of love
     From each to each
   Trembles a rarer speech,
And with its presence every pause doth fill.

Unmoved it broods, this all-encompassing hush
   Of one who stooping near,
   No smallest stir will make
     Our fear to wake;
     But yet intent
   Upon some mystery bent,
Hearkens the lightest word we say, or hear.

# Winter Dusk

Dark frost was in the air without,
The dusk was still with cold and gloom,
When less than even a shadow came
   And stood within the room.

But of the three around the fire,
None turned a questioning head to look,
Still read a clear voice, on and on,
   Still stooped they o'er their book.

The children watched their mother's eyes
Moving on softly line to line;
It seemed to listen too—that shade,
   Yet made no outward sign.

The fire-flames crooned a tiny song,
No cold wind moved the wintry tree;
The children both in Faërie dreamed
   Beside their mother's knee.

And nearer yet that spirit drew
Above that heedless one, intent
Only on what the simple words
   Of her small story meant.

No voiceless sorrow grieved her mind,
No memory her bosom stirred,
Nor dreamed she, as she read to two,
   'Twas surely three who heard.

Yet when, the story done, she smiled
From face to face, serene and clear,
A love, half dread, sprang up, as she
    Leaned close and drew them near.

# Ages Ago

Launcelot loved Guinevere,
　　Ages and ages ago,
Beautiful as a bird was she,
Preening its wings in a cypress tree,
Happy in sadness, she and he,
　　They loved each other so.

Helen of Troy was beautiful
　　As tender flower in May,
Her loveliness from the towers looked down,
With the sweet moon for silver crown,
Over the walls of Troy Town,
　　Hundreds of years away.

Cleopatra, Egypt's Queen,
　　Was wondrous kind to ken,
As when the stars in the dark sky
Like buds on thorny branches lie,
So seemed she too to Antony,
　　That age-gone prince of men.

The Pyramids are old stones,
　　Scarred is that grey face,
That by the greenness of Old Nile
Gazes with an unchanging smile,
Man with all mystery to beguile
　　And give his thinking grace.

# Home

Rest, rest—there is no rest,
Until the quiet grave
Comes with its narrow arch
   The heart to save
From life's long cankering rust,
From torpor, cold and still—
The loveless, saddened dust,
   The jaded will.

And yet, be far the hour
Whose haven calls me home;
Long be the arduous day
   Till evening come;
What sureness now remains
But that through livelong strife
Only the loser gains
   An end to life?

Then in the soundless deep
Of even the shallowest grave
Childhood and love he'll keep,
   And his soul save;
All vext desire, all vain
Cries of a conflict done
Fallen to rest again;
   Death's refuge won.

# The Ghost

Peace in thy hands,
Peace in thine eyes,
Peace on thy brow;
Flower of a moment in the eternal hour,
Peace with me now.

Not a wave breaks,
Not a bird calls,
My heart, like a sea,
Silent after a storm that hath died,
Sleeps within me.

All the night's dews,
All the world's leaves,
All winter's snow
Seem with their quiet to have stilled in life's dream
All sorrowing now.

# An Epitaph

Here lies a most beautiful lady,
Light of step and heart was she;
I think she was the most beautiful lady
That ever was in the West Country.
But beauty vanishes; beauty passes;
However rare—rare it be;
And when I crumble, who will remember
This lady of the West Country?

# 'The Hawthorn hath a Deathly Smell'

The flowers of the field
    Have a sweet smell;
Meadowsweet, tansy, thyme,
    And faint-heart pimpernel;
But sweeter even than these,
    The silver of the may
Wreathed is with incense for
    The Judgment Day.

An apple, a child, dust,
    When falls the evening rain,
Wild briar's spiced leaves,
    Breathe memories again;
With further memory fraught,
    The silver of the may
Wreathed is with incense for
    The Judgment Day.

Eyes of all loveliness—
    Shadow of strange delight,
Even as a flower fades
    Must thou from sight;
But oh, o'er thy grave's mound,
    Till come the Judgment Day,
Wreathed shall with incense be
    Thy sharp-thorned may.